TOOLS FOR CAREGIVERS

- **F&P LEVEL:** B
- **WORD COUNT:** 24
- **CURRICULUM CONNECTIONS:** animals, habitats, nature

Skills to Teach

- **HIGH-FREQUENCY WORDS:** a, has, I, it, see
- **CONTENT WORDS:** beak, bird, crest, feathers, pretty, train, wings
- **PUNCTUATION:** exclamation point, periods
- **WORD STUDY:** /k/, spelled c (crest); long /a/, spelled ai (train); long /e/, spelled ea (beak); long /e/, spelled ee (see); long /e/, spelled y (pretty)
- **TEXT TYPE:** information report

Before Reading Activities

- Read the title and give a simple statement of the main idea.
- Have students "walk" through the book and talk about what they see in the pictures.
- Introduce new vocabulary by having students predict the first letter and locate the word in the text.
- Discuss any unfamiliar concepts that are in the text.

After Reading Activities

Peacocks are very colorful birds. Flip to pages 10–11 with readers. What colors do they see in the peacock feathers? Can readers name other colorful birds, such as parrots or cardinals? Show them images of the examples they list. Then ask them to draw and color their favorite colorful bird.

Tadpole Books are published by Jump!, 5357 Penn Avenue South, Minneapolis, MN 55419, www.jumplibrary.com

Copyright ©2024 Jump. International copyright reserved in all countries. No part of this book may be reproduced in any form without written permission from the publisher.

Editor: Jenna Gleisner **Designer:** Emma Almgren-Bersie

Photo Credits: Eric Isselee/Shutterstock, cover; Potapov Alexander/Shutterstock, 1; ErickPHOTOPRO/Shutterstock, 2tl, 6–7; robertharding/Alamy, 2tr, 3; tristan tan/Shutterstock, 2ml, 8–9; xijian/iStock, 2mr, 10–11; a_v_d/Shutterstock, 2bl, 12–13; Dinal Samarasinghe/Alamy, 2br, 4–5; fotolinchen/iStock, 14–15; Hans Harms/iStock, 16.

Library of Congress Cataloging-in-Publication Data
Names: Deniston, Natalie, author.
Title: Peacocks / by Natalie Deniston.
Description: Minneapolis, MN: Jump!, Inc., [2024]
Series: My first animal books | Includes index.
Audience: Ages 3–6
Identifiers: LCCN 2023024645 (print)
LCCN 2023024646 (ebook)
ISBN 9798889965800 (hardcover)
ISBN 9798889965817 (paperback)
ISBN 9798889965824 (ebook)
Subjects: LCSH: Peafowl—Juvenile literature.
Classification: LCC QL696.G27 D76 2024 (print)
LCC QL696.G27 (ebook)
DDC 598.6/258—dc23/eng/20230525
LC record available at https://lccn.loc.gov/2023024645
LC ebook record available at https://lccn.loc.gov/2023024646

MY FIRST ANIMAL BOOKS

PEACOCKS

by Natalie Deniston

TABLE OF CONTENTS

Words to Know..................................2

Peacocks...............................3

Let's Review!.........................16

Index..................................16

WORDS TO KNOW

beak

bird

crest

feathers

train

wings

PEACOCKS

I see a bird.

wing

It has wings.

beak

It has a beak.

crest

It has a crest.

It has a train.

Pretty!

LET'S REVIEW!

Peacocks are birds with many colors. Point to and name the colors you see below.

INDEX

beak 7
bird 3
crest 9

feathers 11
train 13
wings 5